LIGHTNING
BOLT
BOOKS™

The Supersmart Dog

Mari Schuh

Lerner Publications ◆ Minneapolis

For Kaiser, Otto, and Big Dog

Lerner Publications Company
A division of Lerner Publishing Group, Inc.
241 First Avenue North
Minneapolis, MN 55401 USA

For reading levels and more information, look up this title at www.lernerbooks.com.

Library of Congress Cataloging-in-Publication Data

Names: Schuh, Mari C., 1975- author.
Title: The supersmart dog / by Mari Schuh.
Description: Minneapolis : Lerner Publications, [2018] | Series: Lightning bolt books.
    Supersmart animals | Audience: Ages 6-9. | Audience: K to grade 3. | Includes bibliographical
    references and index.
Identifiers: LCCN 2017038562 (print) | LCCN 2017041139 (ebook) | ISBN 9781541525290 (eb
    pdf) | ISBN 9781541519855 (lb : alk. paper) | ISBN 9781541527607 (pb : alk. paper)
Subjects: LCSH: Dogs—Behavior—Juvenile literature. | Working dogs—Juvenile literature.
Classification: LCC SF433 (print) | LCC SF433 .S3775 2018 (ebook) | DDC 636.7—dc23

LC record available at https://lccn.loc.gov/2017038562

Manufactured in the United States of America
1-44321-34567-11/9/2017

Table of Contents

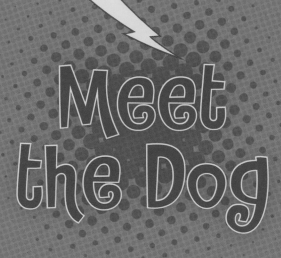

Meet the Dog

A poodle full of energy leaps across a room. A guide dog safely leads its owner down the sidewalk. A course full of tunnels, ramps, and poles is no match for a trained golden retriever.

Border collies are some of the smartest dogs.

Dogs do amazing things every day. People train dogs to follow commands. Dogs help people and can learn to do tricks. They are supersmart animals!

Smart Dogs

Dogs are smart in many different ways. Some are good at keeping their owners safe. Others learn quickly and are easy to train.

Dog toys can be fun
challenges for dogs.

Dogs can learn to find
things, such as treats hidden
in toys. Treats reward dogs
for being smart.

Dogs can use their smarts to help people too. Some dogs work as hunting or herding dogs. Others serve as police dogs or therapy dogs.

Herding dogs help farmers keep track of large groups of farm animals.

This dog is telling its owner that it needs to go outside.

Dogs communicate with people. Supersmart dogs understand when people point and give directions. Dogs use different barks and growls to let people know what they want.

People train dogs to do tricks. These pets learn the names of objects. Some dogs even learn more than 150 words!

Supersmart dogs can count small numbers. Hunting dogs count how many birds they have found. They can also do simple adding and subtracting.

Some dogs can count up to four or five objects.

The Life of a Dog

Dogs can be many shapes and sizes, but they all begin life as tiny puppies. Small female dogs usually have two or three puppies at a time. Large females can have litters of ten or twelve puppies.

Puppies drink their mother's milk for one to two months. Then the puppies eat dog food three or four times a day as they grow. When they are about six months old, they eat twice a day.

Young puppies need to eat more often, but most adult dogs eat twice a day.

This Chihuahua is very small.

Dogs grow to be different sizes. Tiny Chihuahuas weigh only 6 pounds (2.7 kg). Big Saint Bernards can weigh about 200 pounds (91 kg)!

Different breeds of dogs live longer than others. Some breeds live for about six years. Other dogs can live for fourteen years or more.

Dog Care

Dogs can be poisoned if they eat things that are bad for them. Chocolate, grapes, and onions can make dogs sick. Pet owners should also keep cleaning products, medicine, and fertilizers away from dogs.

Dogs can find small items around a home. They can choke on toys such as Legos, batteries, and rubber bands. Pet owners should make sure dogs stay safe by keeping small items where dogs can't reach them.

Hot weather can be bad for dogs too. They can get too hot and thirsty. Keep dogs out of hot cars in the summer.

Dog owners need to be sure their pets have plenty of fresh water to drink.

Pet owners must keep their dogs safe. If a dog gets sick, the dog's owner takes it to the vet. These supersmart pets depend on their owners to keep them healthy and safe.

Dog Diagram

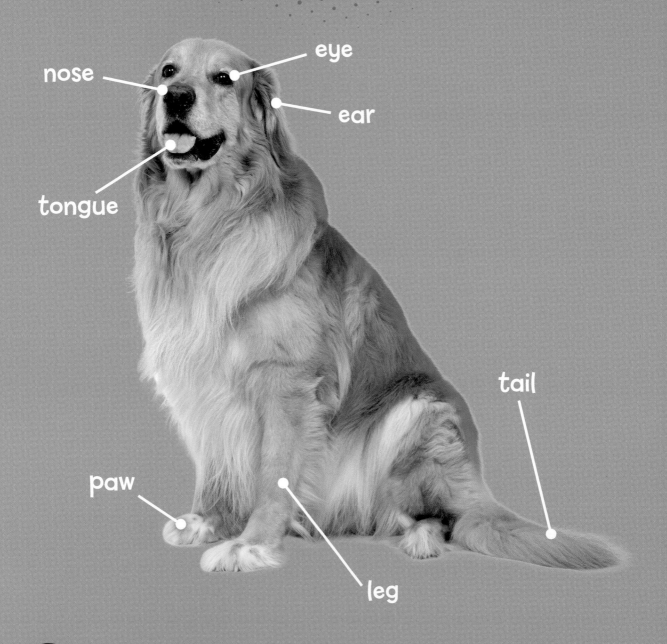

nose

eye

ear

tongue

paw

leg

tail

Fun Facts

- A dog named Chaser is often called the smartest dog in the world. She knows the most words of any dog. Chaser understands more than one thousand words.

- Dogs can learn to do a variety of dance moves, including spins, twists, and jumps.

- Dogs have saved people from danger in many ways. Dogs have helped dig out people who were buried in snow and saved people from drowning and from fires.

Glossary

breed: a type of dog. There are more than four hundred different dog breeds.

command: an order, or direction

communicate: to pass along thoughts, feelings, or information

fertilizer: a substance used to make plants and crops grow better

herding: gathering animals to keep them together

litter: a group of animals that are born at the same time to the same mother

poisoned: to be harmed or killed by a dangerous substance

train: to learn and practice new skills

vet: a doctor who takes care of sick and injured animals

Further Reading

American Kennel Club: Kids and Juniors
https://www.apps.akc.org/apps/kids_juniors/

Ducksters: Dogs
http://www.ducksters.com/animals/dogs.php

Fishman, Jon M. *Hero Military Dogs*. Minneapolis: Lerner Publications, 2017.

Jacobs, Pat. *Dog Pals*. New York: Crabtree, 2018.

Oldfield, Dawn Bluemel. *Police Dogs*. New York: Bearport, 2014.

Science Kids: Fun Dog Facts for Kids
http://www.sciencekids.co.nz/sciencefacts/animals/dog.html

Index

Photo Acknowledgments

The images in this book are used with the permission of: Eric Isselee/Shutterstock.com, pp. 2, 15; Lois McCleary/Shutterstock.com, p. 4; absolutimages/Shutterstock.com, p. 5; michaeljung/Shutterstock.com, p. 6; anetapics/Shutterstock.com, p. 7; Mikkel Bigandt/Shutterstock.com, p. 8; Africa Studio/Shutterstock.com, p. 9; Barbara Peacock/The Image Bank/Getty Images, p. 10; Ewais/Shutterstock.com, pp. 11, 23; Ermolaev Alexander/Shutterstock.com, p. 12; cynoclub/Shutterstock.com, p. 13; Athiporn Phumnicom/Shutterstock.com, p. 14; 135pixels/Shutterstock.com, p. 16; Angelus_Svetlana/Shutterstock.com, p. 17; Helder Almeida/Shutterstock.com, p. 18; ESB Professional/Shutterstock.com, p. 19; jaroslava V/Shutterstock.com, p. 20.

Front cover: Angelique van Heertum/Shutterstock.com.

Main body text set in Billy Infant regular 28/36. Typeface provided by SparkType.

24